LET'S VISIT SAN MARINO

Let's visit SAN MARINO

NOEL CARRICK

ACKNOWLEDGEMENTS

The Author and Publishers are grateful to the following organizations and individuals
for permission to reproduce copyright illustrations in this book:

AGE Fotostock; The Greg Evans Photo Library; Studio Tan.

First published 1988

Published by
MACMILLAN PUBLISHERS LTD
Houndmills, Basingstoke, Hampshire RG21 2XS
and London
Companies and representatives
throughout the world

Designed and produced by Burke Publishing Company Limited
Pegasus House, 116-120 Golden Lane
London EC1Y 0TL, England.

Printed in Hong Kong

British Library Cataloguing in Publication Data
Carrick, Noel
Let's visit San Marino.—(Let's visit).
1.   San Marino—Social life and customs—
Juvenile literature
I.   Title
945'.49   DG975.S2
ISBN 0-333-45519-3

Contents

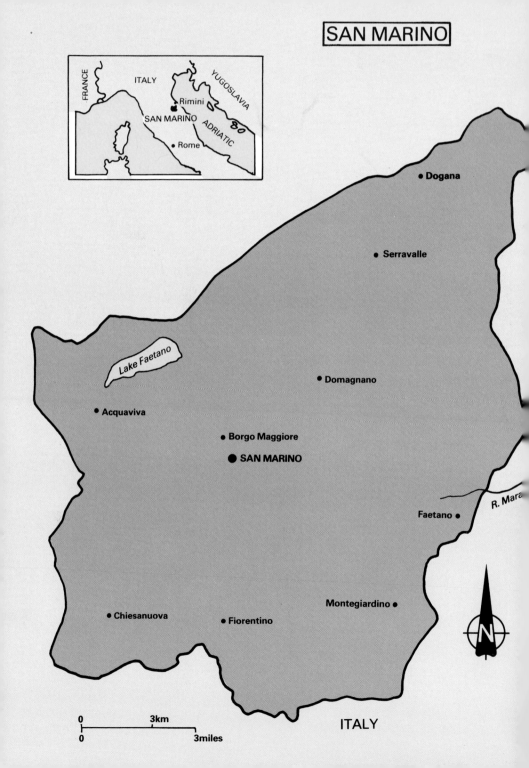

SAN MARINO

FRANCE
ITALY
YUGOSLAVIA
Rimini
SAN MARINO
ADRIATIC
Rome

● Dogana

● Serravalle

Lake Faetano

● Domagnano

● Acquaviva

● Borgo Maggiore

● SAN MARINO

R. Mara

Faetano ●

Montegiardino ●

● Chiesanuova

● Fiorentino

N

ITALY

0   3km
0   3miles

The Smallest Independent Republic in the World

The Republic of San Marino claims to be the smallest independent republic in the world. It is also said that San Marino has existed as a nation for longer than most other countries. Indeed, its origins can be traced back to AD 301. San Marino is completely surrounded by Italy and lies about twenty-two kilometres (thirteen miles) inland from the Italian city of Rimini on the Adriatic coast. The republic occupies the crest and lower slopes of Mount Titano, and has a total area of just 60.5 square kilometres (23 square miles). It has a population of 22,000, and is one of the most densely populated countries in the world, with more than 332 people per square kilometre (860 per square mile). This greatly exceeds the average population of the twelve nations of the European Economic Community, which is 142 per square kilometre (367 per square mile).

Mount Titano has three main peaks on each of which stands an ancient fortress. According to legend, the mountain, which is 750 metres (2,460 feet) high, was named after the Titans—

The jagged Mount Titano with its three peaks, each one topped by an ancient fortress. It makes up much of San Marino's territory

characters from Roman mythology who wanted to remove the great god Jupiter from his throne in the sky. In order to climb up and reach him, they had to place one mountain on top of another. The fact that Mount Titano is so rugged, and therefore easy to defend, has played an important part in the country's history. Of all the small, independent states which once existed in the area now known as the modern country of Italy, San Marino is the only one to have remained free and independent.

At its widest point, San Marino is just nine kilometres (five and a half miles) across and thirteen kilometres (eight miles) long. Its capital, which is little more than a village, is also called San Marino, and is perched on top of Mount Titano. Eight other villages occupy the lower slopes.

The people of San Marino are called Sammarinese. Apart from the country's 22,000 residents, a further 16,000 Sammarinese live in other countries, such as Italy, France, Switzerland, Belgium, Argentina and the United States of America.

Each year San Marino welcomes over three million tourists. The exact number is unknown as tourists are not counted as they cross the frontier. However, even this figure means that there is an average of 136 visitors per year for every inhabitant. San Marino makes its living largely from the tourists who swarm over the border in buses and cars. There are no frontier formalities and many visitors cross into the country without being aware of it. However, San Marino is no fairy-tale land. For more than one thousand years its citizens have enjoyed the kind of civil rights which the inhabitants of other European countries have acquired only in the last century.

San Marino evolved in a different way from the other tiny states which made up the Italian peninsula between the fall of the Roman Empire and the rise of Italy as an independent nation late in the nineteenth century. This was largely due to the geographical location of the country. Surrounded by hills, Mount Titano is predominantly a gigantic seam of limestone resting on a layer of clay which once formed the bed of an ancient sea. Its three peaks, which all have commanding views of the countryside right down to the coast, have been heavily fortified since early times. The natural rock bastions, together with an incredible series of towers, walls, ditches and other defences, have made San Marino a virtually impenetrable fortress for hundreds of years.

Although these unusual geological features have helped the Sammarinese defend their land, they have also been subject to a very slow rise and fall of the earth's crust. This causes buildings to sag and roads to split. The movement of the earth's crust in this region is not great—about half a millimetre (one-fiftieth of an inch) per year—but it is enough to make some of the most important buildings in the republic lean to one side.

Another factor which helped the Sammarinese defend their country was the continual availability of water. During times of peace, supplies were drawn from the two rivers, the Marano and the Ausa, which flow through the republic. However, during less settled periods, the Sammarinese could rely for a constant supply of fresh water on several deep wells within the fortresses high up Mount Titano. These wells enabled defenders to resist a siege for longer than most other forts. They continued to be used by the citizens of San Marino until comparatively recent times.

The mild climate has also contributed to the survival of San Marino. It is unusual for summer temperatures to rise beyond 26 degrees Celsius (78 degrees Fahrenheit). This is in marked contrast to parts of Italy, where temperatures soar well above 40 degrees Celsius (100 degrees Fahrenheit) in the summer months. The clean, dry but cool air in summer gives San Marino a balmy atmosphere. In winter, the capital of San Marino is fortunate enough to be protected from the cold north

La Guaita, one of the fortified towers built on Mount Titano, which has helped to uphold the independence of San Marino

wind by Mount Titano, with the result that temperatures very rarely fall below minus 7 degrees Celsius (19 degrees Fahrenheit).

The history of San Marino, its geography and its political evolution certainly make it an unusual nation. So too does the determination of its inhabitants who have succeeded, against

11

huge odds, in remaining independent. However, more remarkable is the fact that San Marino actually has a double! In the American state of California there is another San Marino, with the same coat of arms, a population almost identical in size and a land area of 62 square kilometres (24 square miles), which is virtually the same as that of its European namesake.

History of San Marino

Founding father, patron saint and national hero—such are the roles of Saint Marino (San Marino in Italian) in the tiny republic that bears his name. According to legend, Saint Marino founded a monastery on top of Mount Titano in AD 301, thereby laying the foundation of the tiny nation of today. Saint Marino, whose name in Latin is *Marinus*—meaning "the man from the sea"—was born on the island of Arbe just off what is now the Dalmatian coast of Yugoslavia. A stonecutter by trade, Saint Marino left his home on Arbe in the hope of finding a better life elsewhere. He crossed the Adriatic Sea to Italy where he worked as a stonecutter in Rimini.

It is not known if Saint Marino came to Italy by choice or if he was sent there as a punishment for his Christian beliefs. However, it is certain that as a devout Christian he would have found life in the largely pagan Roman Empire difficult and frustrating. Indeed, he arrived in Italy during the reign of

13

Emperor Diocletian, who was renowned for his ruthless persecution of Christians. It was to escape such persecutions that Saint Marino and another devout Christian took to the hills. Saint Marino established himself as a hermit on one of the three peaks of Mount Titano, while his companion went to nearby Mount Feretrio, where the famous monastery bearing his name—Saint Leo—still exists.

According to one anonymous author writing in the eleventh

A nineteenth-century engraving of Saint Marino, the founding father of the republic. In his left hand he carries a scroll bearing the word *Libertas* ("freedom") and depicting the three peaks of Mount Titano crowned by towers

century, Mount Titano was at that time surrounded by dense forest inhabited by wild animals, such as boars, wolves and bears. The same author also claimed that the forest contained elephants, which suggests that he might have been prone to exaggeration! However, the steepness of the summit of Mount Titano alone would have ensured that the hermit could go about his daily labour and prayer in solitude.

In time, a group of other pious men gathered around Saint Marino and the first monastic community was formed. The monks obtained formal ownership of Mount Titano as a result of a miracle performed by Saint Marino. According to legend, a boy called Verissimo (the son of a wealthy woman who owned the mountain) encountered the saint as he emerged from a small chapel. The boy aimed an arrow at Saint Marino but, as he was about to shoot, he was suddenly struck by paralysis. When Verissimo's mother, Felicita, learned of her son's plight, she begged Saint Marino to cure him. This was done. In gratitude, Felicita, her son and fifty-one others became Christians—and the mountain was given to Saint Marino.

Saint Marino died in AD 366, sixty-five years after he founded his monastery, and he is buried in the main church of San Marino. His last words were reported as being, ''I leave you free from domination by other men''. Indeed, this still applies to the republic today.

There is no actual proof that the stories and legends about the saint are true. However, a letter written to a cleric in AD 511 by a monk called Eugippio, indicates that the mountain

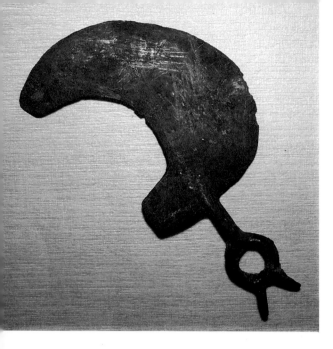

A bronze razor, found in San Marino, dating from around the ninth century BC

was in fact called Mount Titano and that a community of monks, shepherds, peasants, artisans, hunters and woodsmen lived there.

THE DISTANT PAST

Saint Marino is the great figure of the republic's history, even though most of the "facts" about him cannot be wholly confirmed.

Even less is known of the events on and around Mount Titano before Saint Marino arrived. Archaeologists examining fragments of flints found in the republic are sure that a prehistoric population lived there, but no traces have been found of prehistoric houses or other buildings. Excavations between two of the major towers on top of the mountain have uncovered

16

some pieces of pottery and other man-made objects. It is certain that, between the ninth and tenth centuries BC, the Villanovian civilization—a highly developed culture originating from an area near the modern Italian city of Bologna—spread over the area that is now San Marino. There are few traces of any fortresses built at this time, which indicates that it was a peaceful epoch.

Historians believe that the area around San Marino may also have come under Etruscan rule. The Etruscans were a mysterious people who ruled much of northern Italy in pre-Roman times and had a complex and highly organized civilization. Rome later extended its imperial rule over the entire district; Roman coins dating back to the time prior to the reign of Augustus, the first Emperor, have been found in San Marino.

A Roman brooch, made of bronze, found in San Marino. The area now known as San Marino was part of the ancient Roman Empire for four hundred years

The Romans ruled the area for four centuries and their Empire was just beginning to enter its long decline at the time when the holy stonecutter from Arbe arrived to found his monastery.

After the death of Saint Marino, the monastery on Mount Titano continued to flourish. The first written evidence of the existence of a monastery independent of outside clerical and political control dates back to AD 885. It consists of a rather torn document called the *Placito Feretrano*. The document relates to an argument between a priest named Stefano, who was abbot of the monastery of San Marino, and Deltone, Bishop of Rimini. Their dispute was over ownership of the monastery on Mount Titano and the surrounding lands. Another cleric, who decided the outcome of the dispute, found that the Bishop of Rimini had never owned the monastery and that the monastery and lands owed no loyalty, religious or civil, to anyone. This document, discovered in the archives of San Marino in 1749, definitely establishes the origins of the present-day nation—and proves beyond doubt its claim to call itself the world's oldest republic.

There are many subsequent documents relating to the development of the republic. One, dated September 26, AD 951 reveals that, at this time, San Marino had a considerable

La Guaita and La Cesta, two of the three towers constructed early in the history of San Marino to assure the mountain state's defence, still stand today and have become an emblem of San Marino

population. The so-called *Diploma di Berengario,* a document written in the same year, indicates that San Marino had already constructed its first fortifications of towers and walls. This points to the emergence of a civil authority.

At this time, this part of Italy consisted of a number of small states which were frequently changing their boundaries and their regimes. All were tyrannies, usually under the control of powerful families, and few people had either a say in how they were ruled or what would today be called civil rights. The Sammarinese were gradually developing a society that was far ahead of its time. In the eleventh century, San Marino developed a system of municipal—or local—government. By a century later, the basic structure of the government, which still exists today, had been formed.

A document of 1244 outlines the form of government. The Sammarinese were ruled by two men, called Consuls in the ancient Roman tradition. No one can be certain of the exact year when the system of electing two Consuls, with equal power, came into force. However, it is known that the system was firmly established by 1244, and the name of every Consul (or Captain Regent as they came to be called), since that date, is listed. Other political institutions gradually came into being, as the rights of the Sammarinese were defined. However, such recognition of personal liberties did not necessarily mean that the people of San Marino always lived in peace.

So great were the dangers from outside that the small community had both to fortify itself and expand its territory

20

if it were to have any chance of survival. Three towers were constructed on the three peaks of Mount Titano, and the mountain state gained the reputation of being impregnable. By the end of the thirteenth century, the territory of San Marino, which had covered only four square kilometres (one and a half square miles) for many centuries, had grown to twenty-six square kilometres (ten square miles). The expansion had taken place peacefully. Nearby lands and castles had been purchased, rather than conquered. To defend their freedom, the Sammarinese formed armed militias to serve under the Captains Regent, and compulsory military service for all men aged between fourteen and sixty was introduced.

San Marino, despite its desire to remain independent, often found itself involved in the rivalry between the Church and the powerful ruling families. On one occasion, in 1247, all Sammarinese citizens were excommunicated (excluded from the Church) together with one of the most powerful bishops of the region. It was two years before Pope Innocent IV revoked the excommunication. Half a century later, the Sammarinese again fought off an attempt by the papacy to bring them under papal control. This was in 1291 when a priest called Teodorico was sent to San Marino to try to persuade the inhabitants to declare themselves subjects of the Pope and to pay taxes to him. At this time and for centuries afterwards, the Pope was not only the head of the Church, but was a powerful monarch and landowner in his own right, ruling over vast territories. The dispute with the Pope was submitted to a famous lawyer from Rimini for a decision. The judge, Palamede, ruled that the Sammarinese were free and independent of the Pope. Despite this judgement, the conflict with the Church continued and broke into open war in 1304. Fighting continued intermittently for many years and it was not until 1463 that the war ended. One significant outcome of this conflict is that the territory of the Republic of San Marino has not changed since.

FIGHT FOR SURVIVAL

Although the territory of San Marino remained intact, the Sammarinese spent the following century continually trying to

Cesare Borgia, who conquered Mount Titano in 1503

prevent greedy neighbours from taking their nation either by force of arms or by political manoeuvring. In 1503, an army led by Cesare Borgia—a member of the famous family which so influenced Italian history—actually conquered Mount Titano and remained there with his soldiers. Although he permitted the political institutions to function, Borgia made some changes. For example, he only allowed the Captains Regent to hold office for three months, so that he could keep stricter control on them. However, after six months Borgia's forces left, and San Marino had another respite until 1543, when neighbouring states hatched a plot to take possession of the republic. On June 4, 1543, an army set out from Rimini divided into two columns, and approached Mount Titano from two directions. Then a strange thing happened. A dense fog descended (an unheard of event in early summer) and one column of soldiers became lost. When dawn broke and the fog lifted, the Sammarinese lookouts in one of the guard towers were able to spot the column and gave the alarm. The city was saved. Six years later, an invasion attempt by another neighbouring state was also foiled.

The Sammarinese decided that although total independence was possible in theory, they risked losing their independence altogether if they had no allies. After the unsuccessful invasion attempt early in 1549, the republic signed a defence treaty with a nobleman called Guidubaldo, Duke of Urbino. He ruled a neighbouring state whose capital was Urbino—a flourishing centre of the arts which is still largely preserved in its medieval

23

form today. However, by 1631, the tiny Republic of San Marino was surrounded by the country known as the Papal States, which consisted of various lands controlled by the Pope. These had expanded over the years into one of the most powerful states of Italy. When the last Duke of Urbino died, his land was also absorbed into the Papal States and the papal authorities declared that San Marino was under its dominion. However, the local people refused to accept this arrangement and continued to govern themselves.

One of the greatest threats to the republic's independence came in 1739. Cardinal Giulio Alberoni, Papal Legate (ambassador) for the Province of Romagna which formed part of the Papal States, tried to incorporate San Marino into the Pope's territory. At first he tried to persuade the Pope that San Marino was a haven for thieves and criminals but the Pope did not believe him. He then said that the Sammarinese people, who at the time were going through a period of internal strife and dissention, wanted to place themselves under papal rule. Without first obtaining authority from the Pope, the cardinal entered the republic, followed a day later by five hundred of his soldiers.

The cardinal organized a church service during which all Sammarinese authorities were to swear allegience to the Pope—but most of them refused. There were savage reprisals, and the houses of many of the patriots were looted. The Sammarinese appealed directly to the Pope who sent another high-ranking prelate (Monsignor Enrico Enriquez, Governor of Perugia) to investigate. He decided that the cardinal had exceeded his authority, and since there had been no intention on the part of the Pope to change the republic's system of government, San Marino was set free. The last papal soldiers left on the feast of Saint Agatha, on February 5, 1740. This date is still celebrated in San Marino with enthusiasm; Saint Agatha has become joint patron saint of the republic alongside its original founder, Saint Marino.

Just over half a century later, when the Sammarinese had resolved many of their internal differences and the country was in a much better state politically and economically, the tiny nation faced the all-conquering armies of Napoleon. They feared that Napoleon would conquer San Marino as easily as he had overcome other independent Italian states which opposed him. Indeed, Napoleon passed close by the republic but taking into account San Marino's history of freedom, he sent a messenger (the famous French mathematician Gaspare Monge) to reassure the Captains Regent and tell them that he would not invade their nation. Monge read a message from Napoleon, part of which said: "It is our duty to preserve San Marino as an example of freedom". Following the final defeat of Napoleon at the Battle of Waterloo in 1815, the Congress of Vienna was called to reshape Europe. This congress drew up a list of European nations, and San Marino was proud to have a place among them.

During the latter half of the nineteenth century, Italy experienced its greatest turmoil since the fall of the Roman

This statue, dedicated to the "Defenders of Freedom", commemorates the victory of the Republic of San Marino over the troops of Cardinal Giulio Alberoni in 1740

Empire. This was the long struggle for Italian unity. Many citizens of San Marino took part in the various battles, but San Marino itself stood aloof from all attempts to include it in the new nation of Italy. However, the republic did play a significant role in achieving Italian unity in that it gave refuge to many hundreds of Italian liberals.

Garibaldi, a leader of the struggle for a unified Italy, took refuge in San Marino in 1849 and managed to escape just before a combined army of Austrians and papal troops surrounded the republic. Italian unity was finally achieved with the establishment of the Kingdom of Italy. In 1862, the new nation and San Marino signed an agreement recognizing the independence, liberty and sovereignty of the republic. From that moment, San Marino's security as an independent nation has been assured.

How the Country is Governed

The government of San Marino, although quite different in structure from that of any other nation, is based on sound democratic principles. The Republic of San Marino is the oldest republic in the world. Unlike most of today's European republics which have changed their mode of government from monarchy to republic comparatively recently, no king or prince has ever ruled San Marino. Since the nation was founded, the citizens themselves—from the humblest to the most noble—have met and discussed how best to regulate their affairs.

The San Marino version of republicanism, although it has undergone many changes in its hundreds of years of history, is still basically the same as it was in the thirteenth century. There are five basic institutions by which San Marino is ruled. They are the Arengo, which is an assembly of the heads of the nation's families; the Grand and General Council, which is the nation's parliament; two Captains Regent who are the elected Heads of State; the Council of the Twelve which hears

28

complaints about any breaches of citizens' rights; and finally, the Congress of State, which holds the executive power with the Captains Regent and is thus the actual government of the republic.

The Arengo is probably the oldest government institution, but the least important today. Originally, the Arengo held all the power. By the beginning of the tenth century, all heads of families met regularly. They elected a rector to chair their meetings and he (together with a Captain of Defence, also elected by the Arengo) supervised the nation's defences. In 1243, the Arengo elected the first two Consuls, or Captains Regent. However, as time passed, it became apparent that the population was simply too large for all the heads of families to attend a meeting. The Arengo decided to delegate its powers to an organization which later became the Grand and General Council. The Arengo, however, still exists and has the power to modify the statutes of the republic and to petition the Captains Regent on behalf of the citizens. Traditionally, the Arengo submits its petitions twice a year, after the Captains Regent are elected. The petitions must be passed by the Captains Regent to the Council and examined within six months.

San Marino's parliament is the Grand and General Council which has sixty members who are elected for a five-year term. Elections are conducted according to a proportional representation system. Any party which can gain slightly less than two per cent of all votes cast is sure of a seat in the Council. Because of this there are many parties, including the Christian

The Council Hall of the Grand and General Council, San Marino's parliament. The painting on the end wall is of Saint Marino, founder of one of the oldest and most democratic republics in the world

Democratic party, the Communist party, two different Socialist parties, a Marxist-Leninist party, and a uniquely local party called Defence of the Republic.

Like any parliament, the Council passes laws and regulations, directly approves treaties and conventions, and appoints diplomatic and consular representatives. In addition, it has powers not usually given to a parliament. It has the right to grant mercy or amnesty to criminals and can appoint government officials and magistrates.

The Council of the Twelve has many traditional powers, such as "defending the rights of widows and orphans". However, its main practical function is that of an ombudsman—a person

30

who protects citizens from unjust actions that a government agency may have taken against them. The Council has the power (if it is satisfied that a citizen has been unjustly treated by the government) to redress the wrong by annulling the government action. The Council also acts as guardian over Sammarinese property and must approve any application by a foreigner to purchase land or buildings within the republic.

The Congress of State is the newest government organization, established as recently as 1945. Its members are called Representatives, with the exception of those who head the Department of Foreign Affairs, the Department of the Interior and the Treasury—they are called Secretaries of State. They

The Hall of the Council of the Twelve, an organization which hears complaints about unjust treatment by government agencies

The two Captains
Regent, San Marino's
joint Heads of State, in
their traditional
uniforms

are not elected but are appointed for five years and can be re-appointed. The ten members of the Congress of State are presided over by the two most powerful persons in the republic—the Captains Regent.

The office of Captain Regent is the most unusual office in the republic. It is also one of the oldest, most democratic and most practical political offices of any nation in the world. The inhabitants of San Marino have discovered over the centuries that the judgement of a Head of State sometimes becomes

32

affected by the power he wields, and he or she may use his power for purposes other than the good of the country. The republicans of San Marino devised a very simple way to curb the ambitions of a Head of State: They have *two* Heads of State, each with equal power, each keeping an eye on the other, and each holding power for a very short time. Every six months, on April 1 and October 1, the Grand and General Council elects two new Captains Regent. They are joint Heads of State, commanders of the army, and presidents of the Grand and General Council, the Council of the Twelve, and the Congress of State. When the term of a Captain Regent is completed, he cannot apply for re-election to the post until three years have elapsed.

The Captains Regent are extremely powerful. This is one of the reasons why their term of office is kept so short. It is they who convene the Grand and General Council, the Council of Twelve, and the Congress of State, and no matter may be discussed by any of these bodies unless the Captains Regent approve. They themselves can take many different decisions on government matters, but each has the right to veto a decision made by the other.

When the Captains Regent reach the end of their term, a special court called the Syndicate of Regency judges their work, and hears citizens' complaints about what they have done, or failed to do, while in office. One of the advantages of the frequent change of Heads of State is that it provides an opportunity for people of different backgrounds to lead their nation. Over the years many eminent, highly educated and intellectual men have held the office. The Captains Regent have ranged from members of the working class through all levels of society. The people of San Marino believe that this diversity of social levels is the very cornerstone of their form of democracy.

Once elected to office, even the humblest Captain Regent is surrounded by the tradition which goes back at least as far as 1244. Records show that in that year Oddone Scariddi and Filippo de Sterpeto were elected. There were probably many Captains Regent before them but their names were not recorded. There are gaps in the records but, from 1360, the names of each pair of Captains Regent have been recorded and they are listed on the walls of one of the government buildings—the Valloni Palace.

The twice-yearly elections of the Captains Regent and the ceremonies which follow are elegant affairs. After their election by the Grand and General Council, the two new Heads of State, wearing their splendid and colourful uniforms, formally receive all those holding high office in the republic. This ceremony takes place in the Valloni Palace. The Captains Regent wear their costumes of rich velvet and silk, mainly black in colour and of the style of the Cinquecento (the period of the Italian Renaissance between 1500 and 1600). They have knee-breeches, black stockings, and velvet shoes with gold buttons. They wear a scarf round their necks, and their wrists are decorated with white cuffs. Over their breeches is a kind of skirt reaching down to mid-thigh, and a velvet cape is thrown over the uniform. On their heads they wear a black velvet beret with ermine edging.

The ceremony which follows the election of the two Captains Regent. Women have had the right to be elected to high office in San Marino since 1973, including the position of Captain Regent

The final but vital item is a short dagger with a golden handle which is formed into likenesses of the two patron saints—Saint Marino and Saint Agatha. After receiving all those holding high office, the Captains Regent lead a procession to the Basilica (cathedral) where they attend Mass—even though they may be communist non-believers. They then return to the palace to be sworn in by the Secretary of State.

Several major reforms of the political institutions were made after the Second World War. Women were given the right to vote in 1960 and the right to hold high office in 1973. Some Sammarinese doubted whether the office of Captain Regent should be open to women; but the majority favoured the reform.

35

A view of Borgo Maggiore, one of San Marino's old fortified villages and also a "castle" or parish for administrative purposes

The first female Captains Regent have been elected and have served with honour and distinction, bringing a new dimension to this ancient office.

As the area of San Marino is so small, it does not need to have local municipal governments in the way larger nations do. However, for local administrative purposes, San Marino is divided into nine regions called "castles". Most of these are established at, or near, a castle or fortification. However, some have no ancient defence construction at all, and are really little more than villages.

Culture

Despite its long history of political independence, San Marino has always been open to the cultural influences of its Italian neighbours. For example, at no time in its history has the republic developed its own language, although there are some typical Sammarinese expressions and words. The Sammarinese

The Basilica del Santo, San Marino's main church

The interior of the Basilica

speak Florentine Italian as their national language but many of the people also speak the local Romagnolo dialect.

Despite the fact that there have been several communist governments since the Second World War, Roman Catholicism is still regarded as the State religion and most local inhabitants give their religion as Catholic. Although the Sammarinese objected to the Popes having territorial control over San Marino, this did not necessarily mean they rejected the Popes' spiritual guidance and control over their religion. Thus the Catholic Church plays a role in the State in that many ceremonies associated with State occasions take place in the Basilica or other churches. The Basilica is the republic's main church and was

38

built in the fourteenth century in neo-classic style. The remains of Saint Marino are venerated in this Basilica.

There are nine Catholic parishes in the republic and all come under the diocese of San Marino. This diocese actually incorporates some areas outside the republic, including the Italian town of Rimini. In the Church of St Peter, near the Basilica, are some steps and a resting-place, believed to have been cut out of the rock by Saint Marino himself. Many people come here to venerate Saint Marino and his companion Saint Leo.

The altar of the Church of St Peter

The school system in San Marino is similar to that in Italy. Students have many privileges such as free transport to and from school. Sammarinese children attend primary and secondary schools in the republic but, because of the country's small size and population, there is no university. Sammarinese students who pass the appropriate examination, which is recognized in Italy, go on to Italian universities or other institutes of higher learning.

The small size of the population also means that another cultural element present in most other nations is missing in San Marino. Although there are magazines and other periodical publications, there are no daily newspapers published in the republic. Nor are there national radio or television stations. Local San Marino news is broadcast by the Italian State radio each day. The people of San Marino also listen to Italian radio and television programmes and read Italian newspapers. A number of small political and trade union periodicals are, however, published in San Marino.

San Marino's long history has left a large legacy of art treasures in the form of paintings, sculptures, religious artefacts, and other precious objects. Unfortunately, the republic has not been able to keep all its art treasures intact; one of the museums, housed in the Valloni Palace, was bombed by the British during the Second World War, apparently by mistake. Many of its treasures were destroyed—but many were lovingly collected from the rubble, restored and replaced in the palace which was

The Valloni Palace after it was accidentally bombed by the British in 1944

rebuilt to look exactly the same as it was before it was bombed. Despite the destruction of 1944, it now again houses many objects relating to the republic, as well as other historical items, some dating back to the Stone Age.

Paintings now housed there include *Saint Philip Neri* by Guercino; *Saint Marino Lifting Up the Republic,* also by Guercino; and *Saint John the Baptist* by Strozzi. It also houses a collection of archaeological artefacts, marine fossils from Mount Titano, Egyptian statues, and other items such as coins and medals. The rebublic's oldest church, the Church of St Francis, was built

41

A painting of Saint Marino by Guercino—one of the many fine paintings on display in the republic's museums and palaces

in the fourteenth century. This also houses some interesting paintings, the most notable being *Il Guercino* by Giovanni Francesco and *l'Alunno* by Niccolo il Liberatore. More paintings can be found in other churches throughout the republic. However, much of the country's artistic heritage is literally in the streets. Dotted all over the town of San Marino are scores of beautiful sculptured figues, ranging from the *Statue of Liberty* in the form of a young woman in medieval battle-dress, to the ultra modern figure by Emilio Greco of another young woman in an athletic pose.

Paintings and sculptures are concrete forms of cultural heritage. Another form which is more practical but equally enduring is the local cuisine. The traditional cuisine of San Marino is similar to that of the Romagna (the surrounding

42

Italian province) but there are some dishes which are particularly popular in the republic. The Sammarinese love to make their own home-made pasta in many different shapes. Some people claim that because of the many foreigners who have come to live in the country, the local cuisine has lost much of its originality. However, several restaurants serve genuine dishes similar to those prepared by the local housewives from ingredients grown in or near the republic. Some typical dishes include *fagioli con le cotiche*—a thick soup of dark beans flavoured

One of the numerous sculptures which grace the streets of San Marino

**Roast pork being sold
on a street stall**

with bacon rind which is traditionally prepared at Christmas;
and *pasta e cece*—a soup of chickpeas and pasta noodles flavoured
with garlic and rosemary. A great favourite is *nidi di rondine*
(swallow's nest)—a delicately-flavoured dish of hollow noodles
filled with smoked ham, cheese and a meat and tomato sauce.
It is covered with white sauce and baked in the oven.

Hunters returning to the villages of San Marino brought back
their catch; often it consisted only of quite simple things like
snails. Still today, these are turned into a delicious dish. They
are boiled in red wine, with tomatoes, and flavoured with fennel.

44

Fennel-flavoured roast rabbit is another favourite. A popular dessert is *bustrengo,* a kind of cake made with breadcrumbs, cornflour, milk, eggs, sugar and raisins. This is traditionally eaten at carnival time. Another favourite is *cacciatello,* a mixture of milk and eggs which is served cold. Yet another is *zuppa di ciliege* which consists of cherries stewed in red wine and sugar and is served between slices of a special bread. Dishes from the surrounding region which are very popular in San Marino are *tagliatelli* (thin strips of pasta); *ravioli* (small square cushions of pasta stuffed with spiced meat, cheese, or minced vegetables); and *lasagna al forno* (strips of pasta, often coloured green with spinach juice, cooked in layers with meat sauce, cheese, tomato sauce and cream).

The Sammarinese wash down this delicious food with their own locally-produced wine. The most famous is *Sangiovese,* a

Harvesting grapes for Sammarinese wine

strong red wine. Other good wines include *Biancale,* a dry white with a very distinctive taste which accompanies fish or chicken dishes, and *Grilet,* a white sparkling naturally fermented wine which is served chilled. The quality of local wines is kept under strict control by the San Marino Wine Association which is a major wine-producer in its own right. The Sammarinese, with their long traditions of good food and wine, often eat outdoors on the very many fine summer evenings.

Sport and Recreation

Although San Marino is an entirely landlocked country, its young people enjoy participating in water sports, such as swimming, yachting, windsurfing and scuba diving, or simply sunbathing on a beach. This is because San Marino is only a short distance from some of Italy's best-known resorts on the Adriatic coast. Some parts of the republic are only ten kilometres (six miles) from the sea as the crow flies, although it is a little further by road. As there are no frontier formalities, it takes the Sammarinese very little time to reach the beaches.

The major traditional sport of San Marino is archery, in which the skill of local bowmen is unsurpassed. Once a dreaded weapon of war, the crossbow is now used for pleasure; competitions and demonstrations are a feature of San Marino life. It takes great strength and skill to be a champion crossbowman. Strength is required, not only to winch back the heavy metal arch of the bow but also to hold the bow itself. Most bows have to be laid on a support to be fired, not only because of the weight but also

47

A local contest. Archery is San Marino's traditional sport. The skill of the crossbowmen is unsurpassed, and attracts many spectators

to ensure accuracy. The main local archery event takes place each year on September 3 when the bowmen gather in the square of the Palazzo Publico. The archers fire their steel-pointed arrows at a target 36 metres (118 feet) away. As the arrow hits the target, it almost buries itself with a resounding thump.

Pistol- and rifle-shooting are as popular in San Marino as they are in Italy. Young Sammarinese also play tennis, basketball, football and baseball. Many of the people, both young and old, enjoy *bocce,* a popular game of bowls, played

48

with heavy metal balls. One reason for its popularity is that it can be played anywhere, as long as the surface is reasonably flat.

All sports facilities in San Marino are controlled by the nation's National Olympic Committee. San Marino also hosts a motoring Grand Prix which is one of the events counted towards the World Formula One championship. However, the republic has a problem in staging the event, as there is no suitable track within the frontiers of San Marino, so the San Marino Grand Prix is held near the neighbouring Italian town of Imola.

San Marino's climate favours outdoor activity. Walking is quite popular, and several well-defined scenic walks are mapped

The San Marino Grand Prix, one of the most famous of the republic's sporting events — although the race is actually held in the nearby Italian town of Imola, since there are no suitable routes through the republic

out. However, for the less energetic, there are many other activities. San Marino has three cinemas which are usually well attended. Because many of the Sammarinese speak more than one language, foreign-language films are frequently shown. Another pleasant pastime for the Sammarinese is to spend summer evenings promenading or sitting at open air or indoor cafés, discussing politics and other current affairs. For those with more cultural tastes, San Marino has several theatres and concert halls. Those who like art and sculpture are well catered for in

Sammarinese enjoying a quiet drink at an open-air café

Lago di Faetano (Lake Faetano)

the museums and churches—and even outdoors where many superb sculptures adorn tiny parks, squares and the streets themselves.

By contrast, many Sammarinese like hunting and fishing. However, except for limited areas within the boundaries of their tiny country, they must cross the frontier into Italy to enjoy these sports. There is one lake in the republic where fish can be caught—Lago di Faetano (Lake Faetano) which abounds with trout, carp and tench.

San Marino and the Outside World

The unique geographical location of San Marino means that, unlike most independent states, it has little use for military institutions. Because it is neutral, it has no army; because it is landlocked, it has no navy; and because it does not have enough territory for an airfield, it has no airforce. In addition, it has no Customs service, only a tiny diplomatic corps, and few business representatives abroad as its trade is mainly in the kinds of commodities that do not need salesmen to sell—tourism, stamps and coins.

There are only two ways of entering San Marino—by road and by helicopter. For many years there was a railway linking San Marino and Rimini, but this was so badly damaged during the Second World War that it was never reconstructed. The only remaining parts of this railway are some tunnels, and a carriage just inside the border. This is used by the San Marino Government Tourist Office as an information centre for visitors.

In an immediate practical sense, San Marino's relations with the outside world mean its relations with Italy—the country by which it is completely surrounded. And its relations with Italy are largely governed by the Convention of Friendship and Goodwill, signed with the Italian Fascist Government of Benito Mussolini in March 1939. Although the Fascists have long since fallen from power in Italy, the treaty still holds good. Under this Convention, the two countries came to an agreement by which San Marino gave up its right to impose Customs duties

Tourists exploring the narrow streets of a San Marino village. The republic depends on tourism for much of its income

on goods entering from Italy. It receives an annual grant from Italy in compensation. Thus, because there are no Customs and immigration controls on the border, unless the visitor travelling in a bus or car is extremely observant, he or she will probably enter San Marino without noticing it. In theory, there is a code of conduct for some categories of visitors. For instance, if a uniformed soldier from another country wishes to enter the republic, he is obliged under San Marino law to hand his weapons to the police and collect them again on leaving the territory. Alternatively, the foreign soldier may ask the Sammarinese police for permission to take his arms over the border.

San Marino's close relationship with Italy has caused some problems and confusion. Probably the most delicate of these concerns the republic's relationship with the European Economic Community (EEC). The Community consists of a group of twelve European nations—Italy, France, West Germany, Belgium, Luxembourg, the Netherlands, Britain, Denmark, Ireland, Greece, Spain and Portugal—which have joined together for mutual benefits in trade.

The republic and the EEC established diplomatic relations in 1983. In the same year, the President of the EEC, Gaston Thorn, paid an official visit to San Marino. The President faced a complicated legal puzzle. Although San Marino was not a member of the Community, the 1939 Convention with Italy made it part of the Customs territory of the EEC. The San Marino government was not happy with this situation, because

San Marino receives neither EEC subsidies on many products it exports (such as wine, meat and wheat under the Common Agricultural Policy) nor the benefits of special trading agreements which the EEC has with some countries. As a result, negotiations began in 1985 between officials of the European Commission (the Brussels-based headquarters of the EEC) and San Marino in an attempt to reach an agreement which would improve San Marino's position.

San Marino is not a member of the United Nations Organization (UNO) but does participate in many of its conferences. It has permanent observer missions at several UN organizations, including the International Labour Office in Geneva. An observer mission means that San Marino representatives can listen and report to their government on the work of these organizations but cannot take part in debates unless invited. Other international organizations in which San Marino participates include the International Court of Justice, the International Red Cross, and the Universal Postal Union. In addition, because the tourist industry is of vital importance to its economy, San Marino is a prominent member of the International Union of Tourist Organizations.

For historical reasons, the republic retains diplomatic relations with Italy, the Vatican, France and Switzerland. For traditional reasons, it also has close contact with the Military Order of Malta. Because it is officially a Catholic country, San Marino's relations with the Vatican are well established. Pope John Paul II visited the republic in 1982.

As San Marino is officially a neutral nation, it has no military alliance or agreement with any other country. The last battle in which it took part was in 1463, although it has been invaded several times since without fighting taking place. San Marino has no army but it does have a nominal military force of eighty men who participate in ceremonial events—and occasionally help the police maintain law and order on special occasions. Its official weapon is a British muzzle-loading nineteenth-century rifle—which gives an indication of its ability to ward off invading forces. However, the republic has the right in times of crisis to call to arms all able-bodied men, and this did happen during the Second World War.

There is one vital area in which San Marino relies largely on outsiders. This is in the administration of justice—for, except in very minor cases, the courts are presided over by Italian judges. The only citizens of San Marino who hear court cases are the Justices of the Peace. However, they can only try minor cases. The republic has its own criminal code; a very modern clear set of laws drawn up in 1974. However, criminal cases are heard by judges from surrounding Italian provinces, and criminals receiving sentences from courts in the republic serve these sentences in Italian prisons. There is no such thing as civil law in the republic. Judges dealing with civil matters must base their judgements on the statutes of 1600, and on communal laws.

While it is simple for a foreigner to enter the territory of the Republic of San Marino, it is extremely difficult for a foreigner to become a citizen. Once a man becomes a citizen of San Marino, it is not possible to lose that citizenship. A person can only become a citizen of San Marino by being born there (providing both their parents are citizens); by becoming naturalized (which is extremely difficult), or by marrying a citizen. A woman can lose her citizenship by marrying a foreigner, but a man cannot. The republic does not recognize that one of its nationals can renounce citizenship by becoming a naturalized citizen of another country.

The Economy

Although tourism forms the greater part of San Marino's economy, some Sammarinese believe that tourists visit the republic for the wrong reasons. Many would prefer the tourists to come and study the museums, and to learn about the nation's fabulous past and its political ideals. They feel that the majority of the three million people who visit each year only come for the novelty of being in the world's smallest republic. They arrive mostly in tourist buses, wander around the narrow streets of the tiny capital city for an hour or two, buy some souvenirs, and then rejoin their buses and leave. The streets are lined with souvenir shops, bars, cafés and ice-cream stalls—all catering for the tourists' immediate needs.

One of the great disappointments to the local people is that few tourists ever see San Marino at its best—by night. The Italian Adriatic Riviera, with its millions of flickering lights from the many resort centres, provides a view which Sammarinese say matches that of Paris from the Eiffel Tower, or even the

A spectacular night-time view of the Italian Adriatic Riviera seen from San Marino

world-famous view of New York from the top of the Empire State Building.

Even though most tourists remain for such a short time, the money they spend provides a solid economic foundation for the tiny nation. Not only those who sell directly to the tourists profit from them. Many craftsmen earn their living by making traditional artefacts which are sold in the shops. A wide variety of handicrafts have been made on the mountain for centuries. These include pottery, leatherwork, paintings, wrought-iron

59

work, artistic ceramic tiles, wood carvings, ready-made clothing, stone carvings, candles and jewellery. A San Marino craft organization supervises the manufacture of all craftwork and ensures that it is of the highest quality.

Pottery and stonework are probably the two oldest crafts practised in San Marino. Pottery and fragments dating back to the tenth century BC have been discovered on archaeological sites in the republic. San Marino's potters still make many traditional medieval shapes but they also rely on the ever-changing whims of taste of the visitors, and frequently adapt their style as world tastes change. Classic shapes are still sold alongside the less aesthetically beautiful re-creations of the three castles in blue china, and red ceramic knights. Of course, stonecutting and carving are the most traditional of all crafts on Mount Titano because the founder himself originally practised these. The ancient art of stone quarrying and cutting has had a far-reaching and beneficial effect on modern San Marino. In addition, most of the spaces now available for car parking were once stone quarries.

Not long ago the mining and working of stone was, together with farming, the main occupation in San Marino. Today, artisans, using a simple mallet and chisel, still create beautiful works of art and shape building stones, friezes, and other items from the white sandstone for which the republic is famous. At one time San Marino had many prosperous quarries from which building stone was extracted, and this stone was used not only within the republic, but also further afield. San Marino itself is a living monument to the skill of its stonemasons and sculptors. Most public and private buildings are still made from local stone which is shaped by the traditional craftsmen whose skill is admired and copied by those in other countries. The streets of San Marino feature many beautiful statues, ancient and modern, which bear witness to the skill of local sculptors.

One of the most unusual industries in the republic is the manufacture of spirits or liqueurs. Although many of the ingredients for these are imported, the drinks themselves are nevertheless true products of San Marino. They include *Queen Bee,* a sweet drink made of whisky and honey; *Ginger Seng* made from the roots of the ginseng plant; and the famous *Tilus,* a liqueur made partly from the truffle (a small black mushroom-

A selection of Sammarinese food and drink, including some of the liqueurs for which the republic is famous, as well as local sausage

like fungus, which is greatly relished in many other parts of Europe).

Prior to the twentieth century, the development of modern industries was held back by a lack of skilled labour in the republic. However, limestone and cement kilns and ceramic factories developed, and gradually other industries were also established. San Marino follows a policy of full employment for its citizens. This means that both the government and the various industries must continue to ensure full production to keep the labour force in work. The modern factories are not on Mount Titano but are situated in the lower-parts of the republic. Their products include paint, synthetic rubber, ceramic tiling and cement.

Whereas in the past, agriculture provided most employment

An olive grove. Although agriculture is now less important to San Marino's economy, there are still several large olive groves in the republic. Their harvests go for family consumption

Harvest-time beneath the jagged cliffs of Mount Titano

and was a major source of income, it is now a comparatively modest contributor to the republic's total economy. At one time, wheat was the major crop, producing 3,200 tonnes of grain per annum. Now wheat production is much less. Today there are less than half the number of farms there were at the turn of the century because farmers have left the land to seek work in the new industrial plants. Nevertheless, the republic still produces its famous wines, has several large olive groves, breeds cattle

63

and grows small amounts of barley, maize, fruit and vegetables. More than sixty-five per cent of San Marino is covered by farmland, pine forests and native woodland. This contrasts with nearly ninety per cent only three decades ago, the additional land having given way to new buildings and other developments.

A flourishing tourist industry, combined with their own hard work and initiative has enabled the Sammarinese to enjoy a high standard of living. As a result, large numbers of local people no longer emigrate to other countries, as they did in the past. The fact that there is, on average, one motor vehicle for each inhabitant is an indication of the living standards of the country.

The Past on Display

San Marino's historic past is on continuous display. It is there for all to see in the form of ancient buildings, monuments and museums. Its living history is apparent in the form of folkloric displays and other events which take place frequently. These include archery contests and flag-waving, which are reminders

A monument to Garibaldi, the Italian revolutionary leader who sought refuge in San Marino in 1849

Present-day flag-bearers of San Marino in their colourful, medieval-style costumes. They are young men who are proud of their heritage

of past military power, and also processions and ceremonies, which mark important events in San Marino's political and religious calendar.

Some of the most spectacular events relate to San Marino's long military history. Among the most unusual are the activities of the republic's band of flag-wavers; a tradition which goes back beyond the Middle Ages. Each flag consists of a wooden staff, usually made of beech, which is 180 centimetres (71 inches) long and weighs about one and a half kilograms (three pounds). The cloth of the huge flag is of silk. In ancient times, the flag-wavers were the standard-bearers and the signallers of the armies. The flag had three purposes in battle. It could be used as a weapon, for the shaft ended in a sharp steel point with which the flag-

66

bearer could defend himself. It could also be used before the battle, to mark the positions allocated to the various sections of the army. However, its most important role was as a means of communication during the confused struggle into which most battles developed. The flag-bearers used a highly complicated series of flag movements, each with a very clear meaning, to send information to each other. They could signal the area where the action was thickest, or where more reinforcements were required. They could order an advance or retreat, or pinpoint where the archers should concentrate their fire. If a flag was in danger of falling into enemy hands—and this could be dangerous as the flag could then be used to send false signals—

A group of flag-bearers demonstrate their considerable skill in waving and signalling with their huge, hand-painted silk flags

the flag-bearer threw the flag to a colleague standing a long distance away.

Today, San Marino has an official corps of forty, comprising twenty-four majors (who are the flag-bearers), twelve drummers and four trumpeters. The way they manoeuvre, throw and catch the cumbersome flags holds the audience breathless. Classic flag movements include the figure of eight, the wheel and the screw. To practise their skills, medieval flagmen organized contests; today's flag demonstrations are a form of these. The flag-wavers perform alone, in pairs, or in small groups of up to fourteen men. San Marino's flag majors wear medieval-style costumes of tights and richly coloured shirts. The flags bear the republic's coat of arms; and, by tradition, they are always hand-painted. For this reason, the flags are very valuable and carefully maintained.

An equally spectacular display of San Marino's traditional folklore is perfomed by its famous crossbowmen. Archery is probably the republic's oldest tradition. There are documents referring to the use of the crossbow on Mount Titano dating back to AD 1339. One of the traditions connected with the twice yearly appointment of the Captains Regent is that each of them has to present, at public expense, a high quality crossbow. They are made of steel and timber and are so heavy and cumbersome that they have to be rested on a stand for loading and firing. It is claimed that an arrow from a powerful crossbow would hit a soldier with the same force—and capacity to kill—as a bullet fired from a modern rifle. Because of the complex nature of their

The *balestrieri*, or crossbowmen, of San Marino

weapons, crossbowmen were compelled by law to train every day. Thus the tradition of target-firing competitions developed, and still exists today. The most important traditional contest is held on September 3 each year. The Sammarinese Crossbowmen's Federation also organizes contests, both at home and in other countries, throughout the year. The *balestrieri*—crossbowmen—wear uniforms including blue tights, a short red smock and a large black hat.

San Marino's military band, which also has a long and proud history, performs at many of the folkloric events. There are five

San Marino's military band, which plays at many of the republic's national festivals and folklore events. It has a long and proud history

official national festivals, all celebrating events of historic importance. They are February 5, the anniversary of the liberation of the republic after the occupation of the forces of Cardinal Alberoni in 1740; March 25, when Sammarinese celebrate the day in 1906 on which the Arengo enabled true democracy to be implemented; April 1 and October 1, the two days in each year on which the Captains Regent take office; and September 3, the feast of Saint Marino, the patron saint and founder of the republic. All these festivities are marked by parades, pomp and ceremony.

As well as the band, other traditional groups can be seen on

70

national holidays. One is the Guards of the Grand and General Council which was formed in 1740. The Guards' main task today is to form a guard of honour for the Captains Regent. They wear a dark nineteenth-century style uniform with a yellow stripe down the trousers and a cocked hat set off by large white and sky-blue feathers. Another group also marked by a colourful uniform, is that of the Guards of the Fortress, also formed in the eighteenth century, to provide security for the fortresses.

The Guards of the Grand and General Council, formed in 1740. Their main task today is to form a guard of honour for the Captains Regent

They traditionally carry muzzle-loading rifles and the officers wear a uniform of red trousers and green tunic.

Even when there are no specific events taking place, the visitor can gain the flavour of the republic's past by visiting a museum displaying historic artefacts. One such museum is the State Archives, housed in the Valloni Palace. This displays many of the ancient documents precious to San Marino's history. Another museum, containing a huge collection of ancient weapons, is housed in the second tower of the Fortress of La Cesta, a thirteenth-century fortress built on Mount Titano's

The Guards of the Fortress

Armour on display in San Marino's firearms museum

highest peak. It can boast a magnificent view as well as the arms collection. There is also a museum of modern arms, founded in 1872; as well as a Firearms Museum in Borgo Maggiore, which contains pieces of light artillery and a collection of magnificent pistols from the sixteenth, seventeenth and eighteenth centuries.

The Capital—and Other Villages

The official name of the capital of the Republic of San Marino is Città di San Marino which is Italian for "City of San Marino". With only 4,500 inhabitants, it is really nothing more than a spectacular village rather than a city or even a town. There are eight other "castles"—now population centres—not all of which were originally fortified. These are Serravalle, Borgo Maggiore, Faetano, Domagnano, Chiesanuova, Acquaviva, Fiorentino and Montegiardino.

The town of Dogana has the largest population in San Marino and is situated on the north-east side of the republic. A visitor entering the republic at Dogana may notice a huge sign stretching across the road. It reads: *Benvenuti nell'Antica Terra della Libertà*, which means "Welcome to the Ancient Land of Liberty".

Città di San Marino remains the most fascinating place in the republic. Europe has many ancient fortified towns, cities and villages, but few are as impressive as this one. Indeed, Città

74

A view of Fiorentino

di San Marino is a wonderful monument to the skill and daring of many generations of Sammarinese who gradually built their capital on the mountain top.

Perhaps the most spectacular features are the three fortified towers which dominate the three peaks of Mount Titano. They are called La Guaita, La Cesta and Il Montale and are still linked by ramparts, walls and other fortifications. Below the tower lies the capital itself, surrounded by traces of three walls, each one featuring magnificent arched gateways, towers and ramparts. Inside the walls are narrow streets, and squares, dating back hundreds of years. Many of these magnificent streets are lined

"Welcome to the Ancient Land of Liberty"—a sign on the border of San Marino at Dogana, the town with the densest population

with souvenir shops which sell a variety of objects not always beautiful or authentic to San Marino. But even this cannot detract from the character of the place. Nothing could spoil this vibrant, living museum of another era. Most of the buildings are in local sandstone, and the skill of the traditional Sammarinese stonecutters is very evident.

The oldest part of Città di San Marino dates from the early twelfth century. One building in the oldest street (Via della Rocca) is called the Amati and was the first seat of the Council. Built before AD 1150 and constructed from huge pieces of stone, it features a magnificent arched doorway. It is one of many buildings in this area dating back at least eight hundred years. Slightly more recent are the remains of the first of the three

76

surrounding walls erected to protect the capital. The first was built in the thirteenth and fourteenth centuries when the centre of the village was perched on the highest part of Mount Titano. Later in the fourteenth century, the capital had grown beyond this wall and a second wall was constructed to protect the new buildings. About two hundred years later, the third wall, which is still intact in many places, was built. The main entrance to Città di San Marino is through St Francis' Gate. This is only for pedestrians and not cars. The gate, set in a huge imposing stone tower, has been restored several times over the

One of the ancient narrow streets in Città di San Marino

centuries. It was named after the nearby Church of St Francis which dates from 1361 and which has also been restored several times.

Like many towns in northern Italy Città di San Marino has a large selection of buildings in original Renaissance style. The Renaissance (the word literally means "rebirth") was the rebirth of ancient arts and culture, including architecture, which began in Italy in the fourteenth century. One of the republic's most

78

important buildings is the Valloni Palace, which was originally built in 1477. It was destroyed by bombing during the Second World War, but was later rebuilt as an exact replica of the original.

Perhaps the most impressive building is the Government Palace on Liberty Square. Buildings surround three sides of Liberty Square. The fourth side overlooks the steep mountainside. This open side of the square provides a magnificent view of the countryside, which reaches to the Apennine Mountains in the distance. The square makes a splendid setting for many ceremonial occasions. In its centre is the San Marino version of the Statue of Liberty. Like the famous Statue of Liberty which stands on Manhattan Island in New York, the statue in San Marino also takes the form of a young woman. It is the work of a famous sculptor named Stefano Galletti, and was erected in 1876 and paid for by an English woman, Otilia Heyroth Wagner. The grateful Sammarinese, despite the fact that they are republicans, rewarded her by giving her the title of Duchess of Acquaviva.

The fortifications which top Mount Titano's three peaks can be seen from almost any approach to the republic. These fortifications feature on the coat of arms, together with the one word national motto: *Libertas*—which means ''Freedom''. Surprisingly for the nation which calls itself the world's oldest republic, the coat of arms is topped by a royal crown. This is the symbol of monarchy which the republic has scorned throughout its long history. The Sammarinese say that the crown is merely a symbol of supreme authority, rather than a form of government.

The three towers dominate the peaks of the mountain. At its foot lies the ancient town of Mercatale, which is part of the castle of Borgo Maggiore. From here it is possible to take an exciting cable-car ride up the mountain-side to Città di San Marino, taking in the glorious view of the surrounding countryside. The passengers have a ninety-second feast of scenic splendour as the car ascends or descends. This means of public

The Statue of Liberty in Liberty Square

The cable car which operates between Borgo Maggiore and Città di San Marino, offering a spectacular view of the surrounding countryside

transport is run by the Sammarinese authorities and is often used by local people. It is also particularly popular with visitors. The other ''castles'' have their own special appeal and can be easily reached by the only other form of public transport—the local bus service. The bus service has two unusual features probably not found elsewhere in the world. Firstly, there are no timetables. This is because buses are designed for local use and not for tourists, and so buses run more frequently at times

81

when the drivers know there will be the greatest number of passengers. The Sammarinese have also resolved the age-old problem of deciding at which age a child must begin to pay an adult fare. In San Marino, any person under one metre (three feet, three inches) tall, child or adult, travels free. Any person over one metre tall pays the full fare.

Many tourists arrive in their own transport, in the form of cars and motorcycles, and San Marino provides twelve different parking areas. Drivers must take note of the overall seventy kilometres (forty-five miles) per hour speed limit. If they exceed this they are fined on the spot, before they have a chance to perform the very simple act of leaving the country to avoid paying.

Stamps and Coins

Many thousands of people all over the world know of the republic, although most have never visited San Marino. This is because they are collectors of either coins or stamps—and San Marino is well known for both. The republic has issued its own stamps since 1877 when a Postal Agreement was signed with

Stamps such as these provide the main source of income for the government of San Marino

Italy. Since that time, the stamps have become famous, not only because of the high quality of their design but also because of the novelty of their themes.

Each year at least five different sets of stamps are produced, and collectors throughout the world subscribe to them regularly. Many older San Marino stamps have become quite valuable. Some of them portray traditional themes, such as the coat of arms, various castles, and of course Saint Marino himself. However, some sets feature less serious motifs. One, for example, bore the likeness of the famous American cartoonist and film-maker, Walt Disney, and some of his most famous cartoon characters including Donald Duck, Micky Mouse and Goofy. San Marino stamps are always designed by well-known artists and are printed not in the republic but in Italy, Switzerland or Austria—or even as far away as Finland. Most sets are sold in huge quantities of up to 750,000 copies.

The Republic of San Marino and the Principality of Liechtenstein (a tiny country sandwiched between Austria and Switzerland) both earn a high proportion of their national income from the sale of stamps. In fact, the sale of postage stamps is the main source of revenue for the government of San Marino. Every stamp ever produced in San Marino is on display in the Philatelic and Numismatic Museum which is housed in a wonderful sixteenth-century building in the Piazza Belzoppi. The museum also contains stamp issues from all nations which are members of the Universal Postal Union.

San Marino's coins are also on show in this museum. Until

REPUBBLICA DI SAN MARINO

SAN MARINO · SAN MARINO · SAN MARINO · SAN MARINO · SAN MARINO

1000   1000   1000   1000   1000

CENTENARIO DEL FRANCOBOLLO

Stamps portraying Saint Marino. The founder is one of the traditional themes in San Marino stamps, which are valued by collectors

1938, San Marino produced its own coinage, although the coins were of the same denominations and size as Italian coins. The currency is the San Marino lira, which has the same value as the Italian lira. Today, most money circulating in the republic is in fact Italian.

San Marino began minting its own coins in 1864. From 1938 until 1971 the republic used Italian coins exclusively. Since 1971, the San Marino lira has again been in circulation. However, there is one serious problem with San Marino lira coins. Visitors keep them as souvenirs and the republic continually has to mint new ones. They do not remain in circulation for the same length

85

The interior of the Philatelic and Numismatic Museum

of time as do coins in other countries. For example, coins which are true collectors' items are gold pieces which are legal tender only within the republic. Most find their way directly into the hands of collectors.

A glimpse at modern San Marino coins provides the reason why so many of them are bought as souvenirs or collectors' items. The 1985 coins, designed by the Italian sculptor Angelo Grilli, are "money with a message"—they depict a problem known all over the world. The nine coins, with face values of between one lira and five hundred lira, all depict the struggle against drug abuse. The coins are of stark design and seem more like miniature sculptures than conventional coins. The theme of the series is "War on Drugs". The first three coins, the lowest denominations, illustrate a person falling into the habit of taking

86

drugs. The five-lira coin, for example, bears the agonized face of a young drug addict. The second three coins illustrate ways of preventing drug addiction, and the last three depict the rescue and restoration of an addict.

While its coins are ultra modern, San Marino's coat of arms, flag and other items of heraldry remain ancient. The coat of arms takes the form of a shield on which are portrayed stylized images of the three mountain peaks, each topped with a fortified tower. These represent the three fortified towers on Mount Titano. Two branches, one laurel and the other oak, flank the shield; and three plumes cap the three towers. The national motto, *Libertas,* is inscribed under the shield. The flag consists of a simple design; two diagonal bands, the upper white and

**The Sammarinese flag
displayed in the
Garibaldi Museum**

the lower blue, over which is placed the coat of arms. The blue stands for liberty and the white for peace.

San Marino's national anthem is probably the oldest anthem of any country. It stems from a monastic chorale dating back to the tenth century. It is a solemn and stirring musical work. Unlike the national anthems of most nations, that of San Marino has no words. However, the very nature of the music is enough to rouse the patriotic emotions of the proud Sammarinese.

The Twentieth Century—and Beyond

Since the beginning of the twentieth century, San Marino has survived a number of political and domestic crises. With each event the Sammarinese have become more confident that their tiny nation will maintain its independence and neutrality. The first crisis occurred at the turn of the century. The Sammarinese call it the "peaceful revolution" because it resulted in a more democratic form of government in which power was granted to an elected parliament known as the Grand and General Council. This was established as a result of protests from many citizens, who at this time faced very serious economic and financial problems. The first elections for the Grand and General Council were held in 1906. The Sammarinese celebrate March 25 as a public holiday. This marks the day in 1906 when the Arengo took the far-sighted decision that in future the members of the Grand and General Council would be democratically elected.

San Marino remained neutral during the First and Second

World Wars. However, many Sammarinese volunteered to join the Italian Army during the First World War and the republic organized a camp hospital to treat the war wounded. San Marino went through a bad economic period shortly after the end of the First World War. At this time, Fascism—which was gaining strength in Italy—spread over its borders. Fascism was a right-wing political movement which used violence rather than more peaceful methods to achieve its ends. Fascism very soon became so strong in San Marino that, in the election of March 1923, the Fascists gained an absolute majority in the Grand and General Council and two Fascist Captains Regent were appointed.

Despite certain sympathies for the Fascist cause, San Marino again maintained its traditional neutrality during the Second World War. However this time the republic did not escape the war. As the Allied armies fought their way from the south to the north of Italy, refugees poured into San Marino, hoping to escape the fighting between the Allied and German forces. It is estimated that, at one time, one hundred thousand refugees (mainly Italians) were in San Marino. Somehow the tiny republic managed to feed and house this vast number of people. Many were housed in public buildings, railway tunnels, or any shelter that could be provided. The strain on the economy of the republic was enormous.

Then, while the refugees were still there, one of the most curious and sad incidents of the Second World War took place. On June 26, 1944, British bombers raided San Marino four times, dropping 243 bombs within the republic's borders, killing sixty-three people and injuring hundreds more. The Sammarinese could not understand why they had been bombed as there were no German troops in the country. The British Government later paid San Marino a large sum of money in compensation for the damage which the Royal Air Force had caused.

The fate of San Marino during the Second World War resulted partially from a policy which it had followed for hundreds of years. No genuine political refugee, nor any person escaping from persecution because of his or her religious beliefs, is ever refused help. Over the centuries, greedy neighbouring states often used this policy as an excuse to attempt to conquer the republic. They claimed that, because of the policy, San Marino housed political conspirators or simply had become a haven for common criminals. But the policy still exists, and the Sammarinese say they will never change their opinions regarding this matter.

After the Second World War, San Marino reacted strongly against the right-wing influence of the 1930s and early 1940s. Indeed, on several occasions during the 1940s and 1950s left-wing governments were elected. However the republic's democratic system of government ensured that left-wing governments could also be voted out.

This tiny state has stood the test of time, triumphing over many crises during the centuries. In terms of its history and its form of government, San Marino is a unique relic. Having preserved its independence and national character for longer than any other existing state, it proudly takes its place among the twentieth-century nations. It is proud of its past, happy with its present, and confident that it has a long future.

Index

93

94